Welcome Baby

Stick your favorite picture here

Guest

My Predictions

Baby's date of birth

Baby weight

Hair color

Name suggestion

Time of birth

Baby height

Eye color

First word

Hours of labor

Advice for Parents

Wishes for Baby

Guest

_____

My Predictions

Baby's date of birth   Time of birth   Hours of labor

Baby weight   Baby height

Hair color   Eye color

Name suggestion   First word

Advice for Parents

_____

_____

Wishes for Baby

_____

_____

Guest

My Predictions

Baby's date of birth

Time of birth

Hours of labor

Baby weight

Baby height

Hair color

Eye color

Name suggestion

First word

Advice for Parents

_____

_____

Wishes for Baby

_____

_____

Guest

_____

My Predictions

Baby's date of birth   Time of birth   Hours of labor

Baby weight   Baby height

Hair color   Eye color

Name suggestion   First word

Advice for Parents

_____

_____

Wishes for Baby

_____

_____

Guest

_____

My Predictions

Baby's date of birth   Time of birth   Hours of labor

Baby weight   Baby height

Hair color   Eye color

Name suggestion   First word

Advice for Parents

_____

_____

Wishes for Baby

_____

_____

Guest

_____

_____

My Predictions

Baby's date of birth   Time of birth   Hours of labor

Baby weight   Baby height

Hair color   Eye color

Name suggestion   First word

Advice for Parents

_____

_____

Wishes for Baby

_____

_____

Guest

My Predictions

Baby's date of birth

Time of birth

Hours of labor

Baby weight

Baby height

Hair color

Eye color

Name suggestion

First word

Advice for Parents

Wishes for Baby

Guest

_____

My Predictions

Baby's date of birth

Baby weight

Hair color

Name suggestion

Time of birth

Baby height

Eye color

First word

Hours of labor

Advice for Parents

_____

_____

Wishes for Baby

_____

_____

Guest

My Predictions

Baby's date of birth

Time of birth

Hours of labor

Baby weight

Baby height

Hair color

Eye color

Name suggestion

First word

Advice for Parents

Wishes for Baby

Guest

My Predictions

Baby's date of birth

Time of birth

Hours of labor

Baby weight

Baby height

Hair color

Eye color

Name suggestion

First word

Advice for Parents

Wishes for Baby

Guest

My Predictions

Baby's date of birth

Time of birth

Hours of labor

Baby weight

Baby height

Hair color

Eye color

Name suggestion

First word

Advice for Parents

Wishes for Baby

Guest

_____

My Predictions

Baby's date of birth   Time of birth   Hours of labor

Baby weight   Baby height

Hair color   Eye color

Name suggestion   First word

Advice for Parents

_____

_____

Wishes for Baby

_____

_____

Guest

My Predictions

Baby's date of birth

Time of birth

Hours of labor

Baby weight

Baby height

Hair color

Eye color

Name suggestion

First word

Advice for Parents

_____

_____

Wishes for Baby

_____

_____

Guest

My Predictions

Baby's date of birth

Time of birth

Hours of labor

Baby weight

Baby height

Hair color

Eye color

Name suggestion

First word

Advice for Parents

Wishes for Baby

Guest

_____

My Predictions

Baby's date of birth   Time of birth   Hours of labor

Baby weight   Baby height

Hair color   Eye color

Name suggestion   First word

Advice for Parents

_____

_____

Wishes for Baby

_____

_____

Guest

My Predictions

Baby's date of birth

Time of birth

Hours of labor

Baby weight

Baby height

Hair color

Eye color

Name suggestion

First word

Advice for Parents

Wishes for Baby

Guest

_____

My Predictions

Baby's date of birth

Time of birth

Hours of labor

Baby weight

Baby height

Hair color

Eye color

Name suggestion

First word

Advice for Parents

_____

_____

Wishes for Baby

_____

_____

Guest

_____

My Predictions

Baby's date of birth   Time of birth   Hours of labor

Baby weight   Baby height

Hair color   Eye color

Name suggestion   First word

Advice for Parents

_____

_____

Wishes for Baby

_____

_____

Guest

My Predictions

Baby's date of birth

Time of birth

Hours of labor

Baby weight

Baby height

Hair color

Eye color

Name suggestion

First word

Advice for Parents

Wishes for Baby

Guest

My Predictions

Baby's date of birth

Time of birth

Hours of labor

Baby weight

Baby height

Hair color

Eye color

Name suggestion

First word

Advice for Parents

Wishes for Baby

Guest

_____

My Predictions

Baby's date of birth

Time of birth

Hours of labor

Baby weight

Baby height

Hair color

Eye color

Name suggestion

First word

Advice for Parents

_____

_____

Wishes for Baby

_____

_____

Guest

_____

My Predictions

Baby's date of birth   Time of birth   Hours of labor

Baby weight   Baby height

Hair color   Eye color

Name suggestion   First word

Advice for Parents

_____

_____

Wishes for Baby

_____

_____

Guest

_____

My Predictions

Baby's date of birth   Time of birth   Hours of labor

Baby weight   Baby height

Hair color   Eye color

Name suggestion   First word

Advice for Parents

_____

_____

Wishes for Baby

_____

_____

Guest

My Predictions

Baby's date of birth

Time of birth

Hours of labor

Baby weight

Baby height

Hair color

Eye color

Name suggestion

First word

Advice for Parents

Wishes for Baby

Guest

My Predictions

Baby's date of birth

Time of birth

Hours of labor

Baby weight

Baby height

Hair color

Eye color

Name suggestion

First word

Advice for Parents

Wishes for Baby

Guest

_____

My Predictions

Baby's date of birth   Time of birth   Hours of labor

Baby weight   Baby height

Hair color   Eye color

Name suggestion   First word

Advice for Parents

_____
_____

Wishes for Baby

_____
_____

Guest

_____

My Predictions

Baby's date of birth

Time of birth

Hours of labor

Baby weight

Baby height

Hair color

Eye color

Name suggestion

First word

Advice for Parents

_____

_____

Wishes for Baby

_____

_____

Guest

My Predictions

Baby's date of birth

Time of birth

Hours of labor

Baby weight

Baby height

Hair color

Eye color

Name suggestion

First word

Advice for Parents

Wishes for Baby

Guest

_____

My Predictions

Baby's date of birth

Baby weight

Hair color

Name suggestion

Time of birth

Baby height

Eye color

First word

Hours of labor

Advice for Parents

_____
_____

Wishes for Baby

_____
_____

Guest

My Predictions

Baby's date of birth

Time of birth

Hours of labor

Baby weight

Baby height

Hair color

Eye color

Name suggestion

First word

Advice for Parents

Wishes for Baby

Guest

_____

My Predictions

Baby's date of birth

Baby weight

Hair color

Name suggestion

Time of birth

Baby height

Eye color

First word

Hours of labor

Advice for Parents

_____

_____

Wishes for Baby

_____

_____

Guest

My Predictions

Baby's date of birth   Time of birth   Hours of labor

Baby weight   Baby height

Hair color   Eye color

Name suggestion   First word

Advice for Parents

Wishes for Baby

Guest

My Predictions

Baby's date of birth

Time of birth

Hours of labor

Baby weight

Baby height

Hair color

Eye color

Name suggestion

First word

Advice for Parents

Wishes for Baby

Guest

_____

My Predictions

Baby's date of birth   Time of birth   Hours of labor

Baby weight   Baby height

Hair color   Eye color

Name suggestion   First word

Advice for Parents

_____

_____

Wishes for Baby

_____

_____

Guest

My Predictions

Baby's date of birth

Baby weight

Hair color

Name suggestion

Time of birth

Baby height

Eye color

First word

Hours of labor

Advice for Parents

Wishes for Baby

Guest

My Predictions

Baby's date of birth

Time of birth

Hours of labor

Baby weight

Baby height

Hair color

Eye color

Name suggestion

First word

Advice for Parents

Wishes for Baby

Guest

_____

My Predictions

Baby's date of birth   Time of birth   Hours of labor

Baby weight   Baby height

Hair color   Eye color

Name suggestion   First word

Advice for Parents

_____

_____

Wishes for Baby

_____

_____

Guest

My Predictions

Baby's date of birth

Time of birth

Hours of labor

Baby weight

Baby height

Hair color

Eye color

Name suggestion

First word

Advice for Parents

Wishes for Baby

Guest

My Predictions

Baby's date of birth

Time of birth

Hours of labor

Baby weight

Baby height

Hair color

Eye color

Name suggestion

First word

Advice for Parents

Wishes for Baby

Guest

My Predictions

Baby's date of birth

Time of birth

Hours of labor

Baby weight

Baby height

Hair color

Eye color

Name suggestion

First word

Advice for Parents

Wishes for Baby

Guest

My Predictions

Baby's date of birth

Time of birth

Hours of labor

Baby weight

Baby height

Hair color

Eye color

Name suggestion

First word

Advice for Parents

Wishes for Baby

Guest

My Predictions

Baby's date of birth

Baby weight

Hair color

Name suggestion

Time of birth

Baby height

Eye color

First word

Hours of labor

Advice for Parents

Wishes for Baby

Guest

My Predictions

Baby's date of birth

Baby weight

Hair color

Name suggestion

Time of birth

Baby height

Eye color

First word

Hours of labor

Advice for Parents

Wishes for Baby

Guest

My Predictions

Baby's date of birth

Time of birth

Hours of labor

Baby weight

Baby height

Hair color

Eye color

Name suggestion

First word

Advice for Parents

Wishes for Baby

Guest

My Predictions

Baby's date of birth

Time of birth

Hours of labor

Baby weight

Baby height

Hair color

Eye color

Name suggestion

First word

Advice for Parents

Wishes for Baby

Guest

My Predictions

Baby's date of birth

Time of birth

Hours of labor

Baby weight

Baby height

Hair color

Eye color

Name suggestion

First word

Advice for Parents

Wishes for Baby

Guest

_____

My Predictions

Baby's date of birth

Time of birth

Hours of labor

Baby weight

Baby height

Hair color

Eye color

Name suggestion

First word

Advice for Parents

_____
_____

Wishes for Baby

_____
_____

Guest

My Predictions

Baby's date of birth	Time of birth	Hours of labor
Baby weight	Baby height	
Hair color	Eye color	
Name suggestion	First word	

Advice for Parents

Wishes for Baby

Guest

My Predictions

Baby's date of birth

Time of birth

Hours of labor

Baby weight

Baby height

Hair color

Eye color

Name suggestion

First word

Advice for Parents

_____

_____

Wishes for Baby

_____

_____

Guest

_____

My Predictions

Baby's date of birth   Time of birth   Hours of labor

Baby weight   Baby height

Hair color   Eye color

Name suggestion   First word

Advice for Parents

_____

_____

Wishes for Baby

_____

_____

Guest

My Predictions

Baby's date of birth

Time of birth

Hours of labor

Baby weight

Baby height

Hair color

Eye color

Name suggestion

First word

Advice for Parents

Wishes for Baby

Guest

My Predictions

Baby's date of birth

Time of birth

Hours of labor

Baby weight

Baby height

Hair color

Eye color

Name suggestion

First word

Advice for Parents

Wishes for Baby

Guest

_____

My Predictions

Baby's date of birth   Time of birth   Hours of labor

Baby weight   Baby height

Hair color   Eye color

Name suggestion   First word

Advice for Parents

_____

_____

Wishes for Baby

_____

_____

Guest

My Predictions

Baby's date of birth

Time of birth

Hours of labor

Baby weight

Baby height

Hair color

Eye color

Name suggestion

First word

Advice for Parents

Wishes for Baby

Guest

My Predictions

Baby's date of birth

Time of birth

Hours of labor

Baby weight

Baby height

Hair color

Eye color

Name suggestion

First word

Advice for Parents

Wishes for Baby

Guest

My Predictions

Baby's date of birth

Time of birth

Hours of labor

Baby weight

Baby height

Hair color

Eye color

Name suggestion

First word

Advice for Parents

Wishes for Baby

Guest

_____

My Predictions

Baby's date of birth

Time of birth

Hours of labor

Baby weight

Baby height

Hair color

Eye color

Name suggestion

First word

Advice for Parents

_____

_____

Wishes for Baby

_____

_____

Guest

My Predictions

Baby's date of birth   Time of birth   Hours of labor

Baby weight   Baby height

Hair color   Eye color

Name suggestion   First word

Advice for Parents

Wishes for Baby

Guest

My Predictions

Baby's date of birth

Time of birth

Hours of labor

Baby weight

Baby height

Hair color

Eye color

Name suggestion

First word

Advice for Parents

_____

_____

Wishes for Baby

_____

_____

Guest

_____

My Predictions

Baby's date of birth   Time of birth   Hours of labor

Baby weight   Baby height

Hair color   Eye color

Name suggestion   First word

Advice for Parents

_____

_____

Wishes for Baby

_____

_____

Guest

My Predictions

Baby's date of birth

Time of birth

Hours of labor

Baby weight

Baby height

Hair color

Eye color

Name suggestion

First word

Advice for Parents

Wishes for Baby

Guest

_____

My Predictions

Baby's date of birth   Time of birth   Hours of labor

Baby weight   Baby height

Hair color   Eye color

Name suggestion   First word

Advice for Parents

_____

_____

Wishes for Baby

_____

_____

Guest

My Predictions

Baby's date of birth

Time of birth

Hours of labor

Baby weight

Baby height

Hair color

Eye color

Name suggestion

First word

Advice for Parents

_____

_____

Wishes for Baby

_____

_____

Guest

My Predictions

Baby's date of birth

Time of birth

Hours of labor

Baby weight

Baby height

Hair color

Eye color

Name suggestion

First word

Advice for Parents

Wishes for Baby

Guest

_____

My Predictions

Baby's date of birth   Time of birth   Hours of labor

Baby weight   Baby height

Hair color   Eye color

Name suggestion   First word

Advice for Parents

_____

_____

Wishes for Baby

_____

_____

Guest

_____

My Predictions

Baby's date of birth   Time of birth   Hours of labor

Baby weight   Baby height

Hair color   Eye color

Name suggestion   First word

Advice for Parents

_____

_____

Wishes for Baby

_____

_____

Guest

My Predictions

Baby's date of birth

Time of birth

Hours of labor

Baby weight

Baby height

Hair color

Eye color

Name suggestion

First word

Advice for Parents

_____

_____

Wishes for Baby

_____

_____

Guest

_____

My Predictions

Baby's date of birth

Baby weight

Hair color

Name suggestion

Time of birth

Baby height

Eye color

First word

Hours of labor

Advice for Parents

_____

_____

Wishes for Baby

_____

_____

Guest

My Predictions

Baby's date of birth

Time of birth

Hours of labor

Baby weight

Baby height

Hair color

Eye color

Name suggestion

First word

Advice for Parents

Wishes for Baby

Guest

My Predictions

Baby's date of birth

Time of birth

Hours of labor

Baby weight

Baby height

Hair color

Eye color

Name suggestion

First word

Advice for Parents

Wishes for Baby

Guest

My Predictions

Baby's date of birth

Time of birth

Hours of labor

Baby weight

Baby height

Hair color

Eye color

Name suggestion

First word

Advice for Parents

Wishes for Baby

Guest

_____

My Predictions

Baby's date of birth   Time of birth   Hours of labor

Baby weight   Baby height

Hair color   Eye color

Name suggestion   First word

Advice for Parents

_____

_____

Wishes for Baby

_____

_____

Guest

My Predictions

Baby's date of birth

Time of birth

Hours of labor

Baby weight

Baby height

Hair color

Eye color

Name suggestion

First word

Advice for Parents

Wishes for Baby

Guest

_____

My Predictions

Baby's date of birth

Time of birth

Hours of labor

Baby weight

Baby height

Hair color

Eye color

Name suggestion

First word

Advice for Parents

_____

_____

Wishes for Baby

_____

_____

Guest

My Predictions

Baby's date of birth

Time of birth

Hours of labor

Baby weight

Baby height

Hair color

Eye color

Name suggestion

First word

Advice for Parents

Wishes for Baby

Guest

My Predictions

Baby's date of birth

Time of birth

Hours of labor

Baby weight

Baby height

Hair color

Eye color

Name suggestion

First word

Advice for Parents

Wishes for Baby

Guest

My Predictions

Baby's date of birth

Time of birth

Hours of labor

Baby weight

Baby height

Hair color

Eye color

Name suggestion

First word

Advice for Parents

Wishes for Baby

Guest

_____

My Predictions

Baby's date of birth   Time of birth   Hours of labor

Baby weight   Baby height

Hair color   Eye color

Name suggestion   First word

Advice for Parents

_____

_____

Wishes for Baby

_____

_____

Guest

_____

My Predictions

Baby's date of birth

Time of birth

Hours of labor

Baby weight

Baby height

Hair color

Eye color

Name suggestion

First word

Advice for Parents

_____

_____

Wishes for Baby

_____

_____

Guest

_____

My Predictions

Baby's date of birth   Time of birth   Hours of labor

Baby weight   Baby height

Hair color   Eye color

Name suggestion   First word

Advice for Parents

_____

_____

Wishes for Baby

_____

_____

Guest

_____

My Predictions

Baby's date of birth

Time of birth

Hours of labor

Baby weight

Baby height

Hair color

Eye color

Name suggestion

First word

Advice for Parents

_____

_____

Wishes for Baby

_____

_____

Guest

_____

My Predictions

Baby's date of birth

Baby weight

Hair color

Name suggestion

Time of birth

Baby height

Eye color

First word

Hours of labor

Advice for Parents

_____
_____

Wishes for Baby

_____
_____

Guest

My Predictions

Baby's date of birth

Time of birth

Hours of labor

Baby weight

Baby height

Hair color

Eye color

Name suggestion

First word

Advice for Parents

Wishes for Baby

Guest

_____

My Predictions

Baby's date of birth   Time of birth   Hours of labor

Baby weight   Baby height

Hair color   Eye color

Name suggestion   First word

Advice for Parents

_____

_____

Wishes for Baby

_____

_____

Guest

_____

My Predictions

Baby's date of birth

Time of birth

Hours of labor

Baby weight

Baby height

Hair color

Eye color

Name suggestion

First word

Advice for Parents

_____

_____

Wishes for Baby

_____

_____

Guest

_____

_____

My Predictions

Baby's date of birth   Time of birth   Hours of labor

Baby weight   Baby height

Hair color   Eye color

Name suggestion   First word

Advice for Parents

_____

_____

Wishes for Baby

_____

_____

Guest

My Predictions

Baby's date of birth

Time of birth

Hours of labor

Baby weight

Baby height

Hair color

Eye color

Name suggestion

First word

Advice for Parents

Wishes for Baby

Guest

_____

My Predictions

Baby's date of birth

Time of birth

Hours of labor

Baby weight

Baby height

Hair color

Eye color

Name suggestion

First word

Advice for Parents

_____

_____

Wishes for Baby

_____

_____

Guest

My Predictions

Baby's date of birth

Time of birth

Hours of labor

Baby weight

Baby height

Hair color

Eye color

Name suggestion

First word

Advice for Parents

_____

_____

Wishes for Baby

_____

_____

Guest

My Predictions

Baby's date of birth

Time of birth

Hours of labor

Baby weight

Baby height

Hair color

Eye color

Name suggestion

First word

Advice for Parents

Wishes for Baby

Guest

_____

My Predictions

Baby's date of birth   Time of birth   Hours of labor

Baby weight   Baby height

Hair color   Eye color

Name suggestion   First word

Advice for Parents

_____

_____

Wishes for Baby

_____

_____

Gift Log

Gifts

Gift	Given By	Thank you note sent

Gifts

Gift	Given By	Thank you note sent

Gifts

Gift	Given By	Thank you note sent

Gifts

Gift	Given By	Thank you note sent

Gifts

Gift	Given By	Thank you note sent

Gifts

Gift	Given By	Thank you note sent

Gifts

Gift	Given By	Thank you note sent

Gifts

Gift	Given By	Thank you note sent
_____	_____	_____
_____	_____	_____
_____	_____	_____
_____	_____	_____
_____	_____	_____
_____	_____	_____
_____	_____	_____
_____	_____	_____
_____	_____	_____
_____	_____	_____
_____	_____	_____

Gifts

Gift	Given By	Thank you note sent

Gifts

Gift	Given By	Thank you note sent